Benedict in Irma
A Teddy bear hurricane party
By Cherish Fultz

We went out to get snacks for work cat food. There are people everywhere, trying to get supplies for the upcoming storm. Gas stations are running empty and bottled water is gone everywhere.

I wanted to take a picture in the empty shelves; but mom thought it would be too dangerous.

This is my first big hurricane. I feel perfectly safe with my family. Whatever happens, I feel like I will

be safe

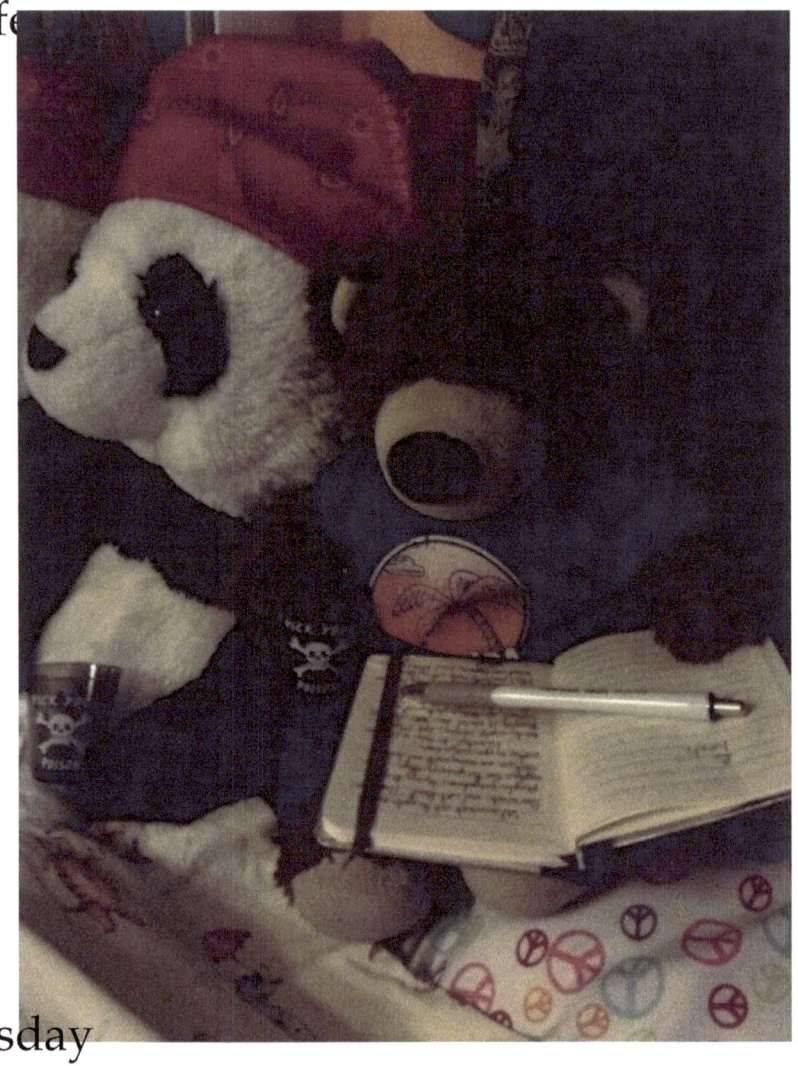

Thursday
9/7/17

We have a CPR class in the morning. Mom did well – she got

everything right. I feel confident that she could help keep the patien

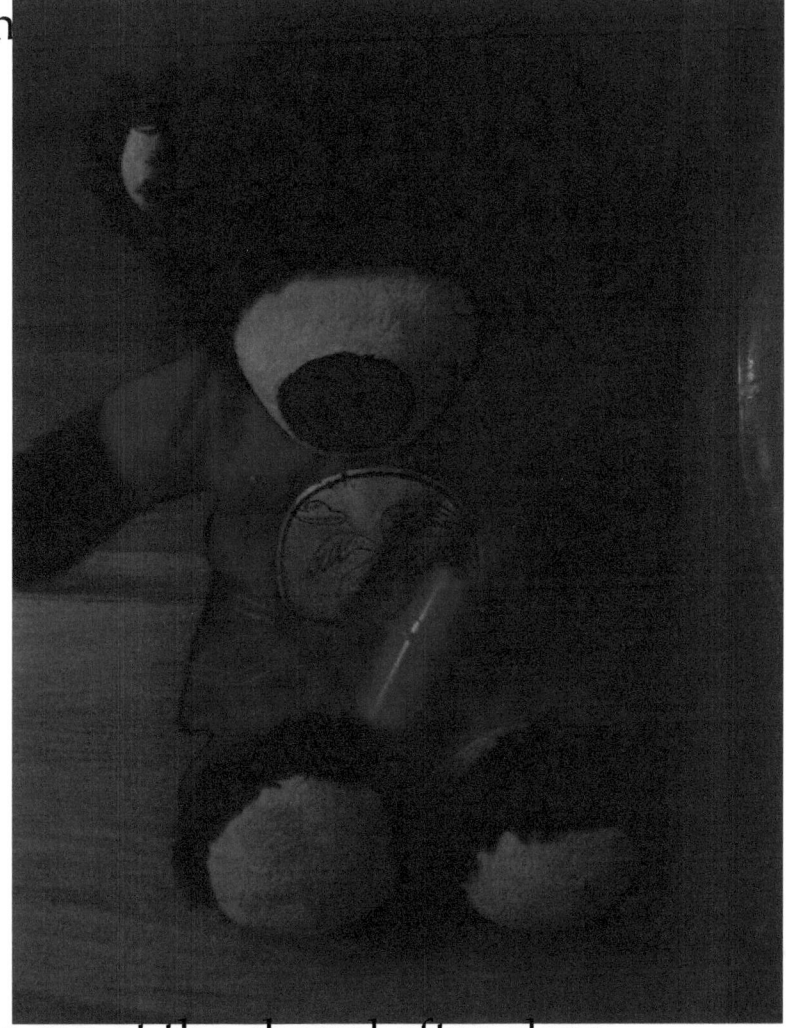

This is me at the chapel after class. The device on my lap with moms on personal breathing tool for the

breathing masks they use for rescue breathing. Everyone gets one to keep, so we don't share germs. I think that is an excellent idea.

I want to turn this thing into a musical instrument if mom will let me. Perhaps with a reed inside it can be like a kazoo. We must not for now, and work tonight.

Friday
9/8/2017

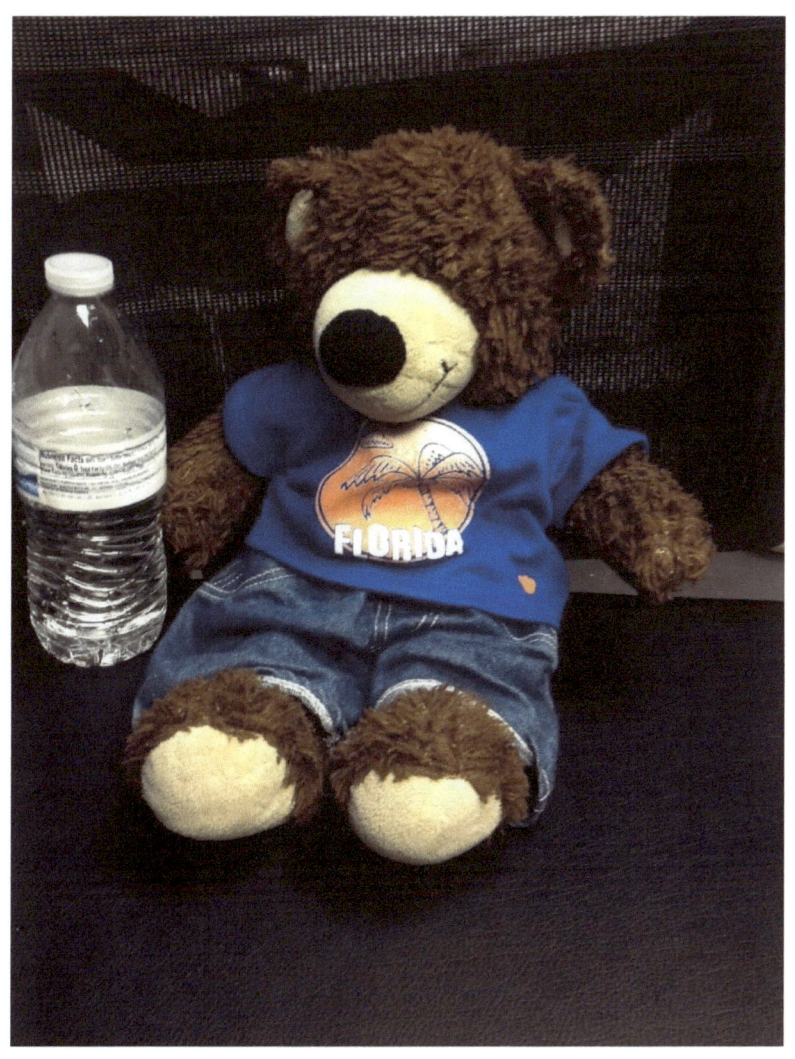

We are at work. We are in a disaster plan, so we might need to stay the night. If we are offered, Mom thinks we will stay. She hates driving in the rain. Driving through a hurricane would be even scarier, especially mom's little Yaris.

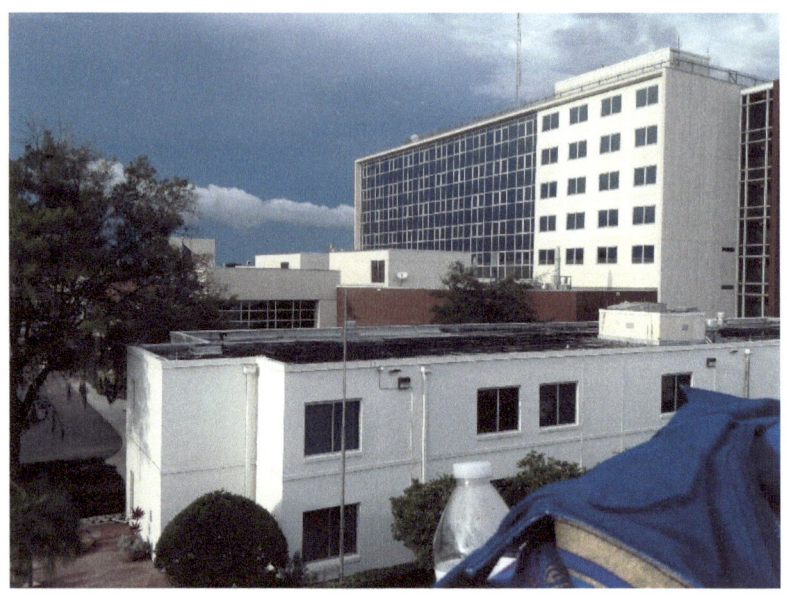

Mom is very excited and anxious. It will be my job to help her keep calm. It is good that I came. Working through hurricane Irma will be an experience like no other.

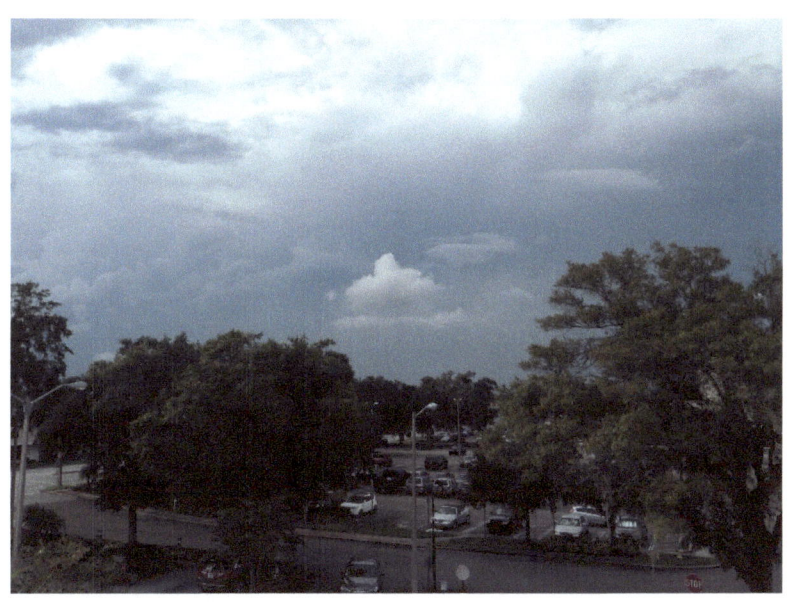

Nana is the one who thought of writing this book and I'm glad she did. Whatever happens, this will be an experience.

Here is a picture of latest trajectory and moms work emails. Since then, is move more to the east, and it should be going over us Sunday night shift – Monday morning about 2 AM.

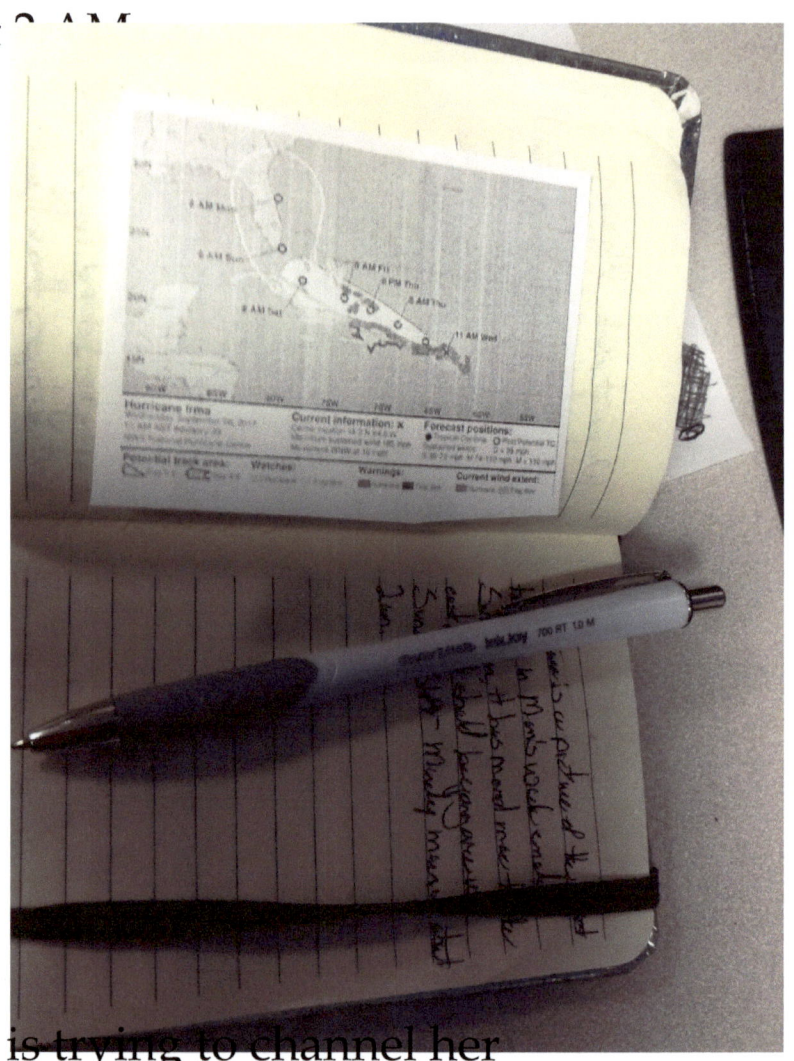

Mom is trying to channel her nervous energy into getting things done at work. I am for whatever works as long as she also takes care of herself. The guys, as usual, seem unflappable.

This is going to be big; especially for little guys like us teddy bears. I hope everyone stays safe is the hurricane passes us by.

Mom is watching the storm live on Facebook. It was going to the right, but now it looks like it's going up through the stadium. People on the cat range from prayerful, to questioning, so pessimistic. Of the three, I choose the prayerful.

All the teddy bears who donated themselves went to Red Cross. Perhaps even now, they're helping the victims of this terrible natural disaster.

Friday
9/8/2017

We came home this morning, not sure what we would do. We woke later to find there was a call from the hospital. It seems that catastrophe time was assigned. We go in normal time tonight, then come in at three tomorrow and stay overnight Saturday and or Sunday. Mom has begun getting her things together this afternoon just in case. It's always good to be prepared; I learned this in bear scouts and Mom in Girl Scouts. She was brownie and I was a cub.

We are at the hospital. It is very

busy. This is the deal. Tomorrow, we check in at 1500 hrs. and stay until Monday. We clock in and out as we work and sleep at the hospital. We will be paid the entire time we have to stay here. Well, Mom will be paid. I am a full-time volunteer. Everyone who works Monday or the weekend have to stay.

We are not guaranteed to bed, so we plan to bring the big quilt, pillow, and a blanket. Thomas is bringing his magic cards, so we need to bring ours. We will bring books to work on and we will take pics for this one.

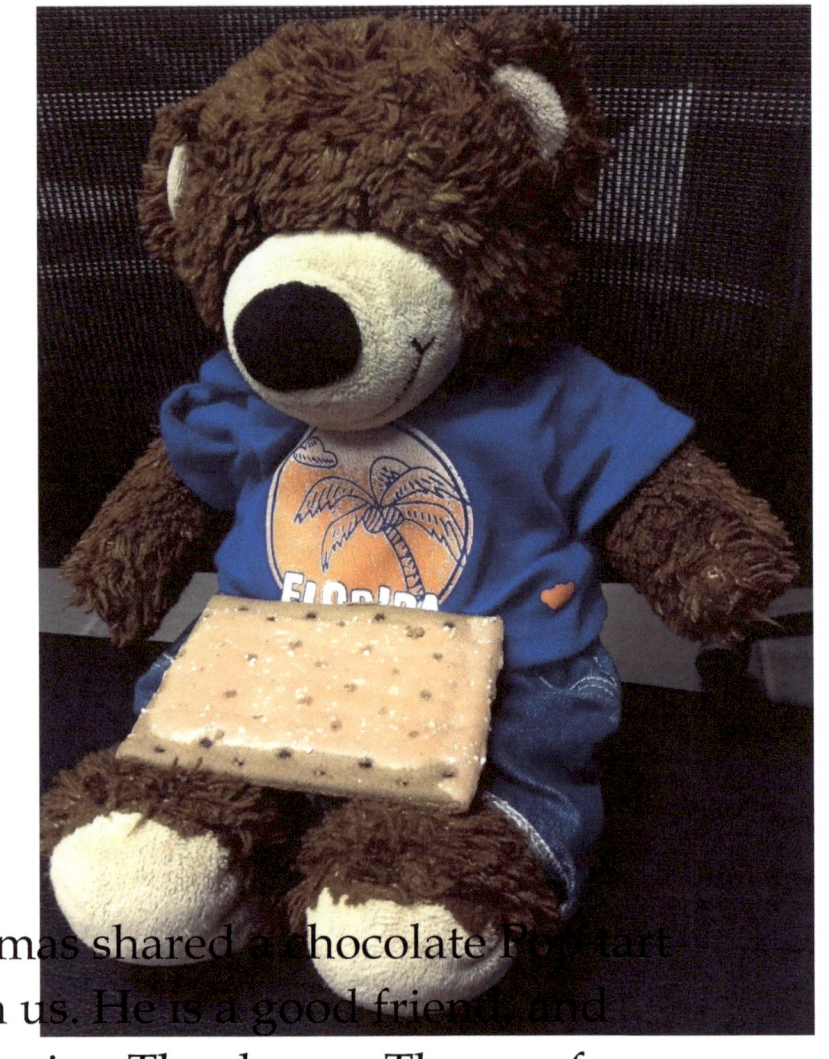

Thomas shared a chocolate Pop tart with us. He is a good friend, and very nice. Thank you, Thomas for the lovely treat.

Everyone comes to talking about the Hurricane. Everyone can feel the anxiety. We are all doing our best to bring a bit of peach to them. Mom is talking over the phone and bright, cheerful tones, and I work to fight the sadness in her heart. Everyone who works at CMU will get assigned in the same area so they will be together day and I for three days, not easy task for any group of humans. I wish them well.

Saturday
9/9/2017

Mom could not sleep, so we came in early. As we arrived, we got a message saying we do not need to come in until five. We are already there last parking space on the second floor, so we came in. Was about 130 in the afternoon.

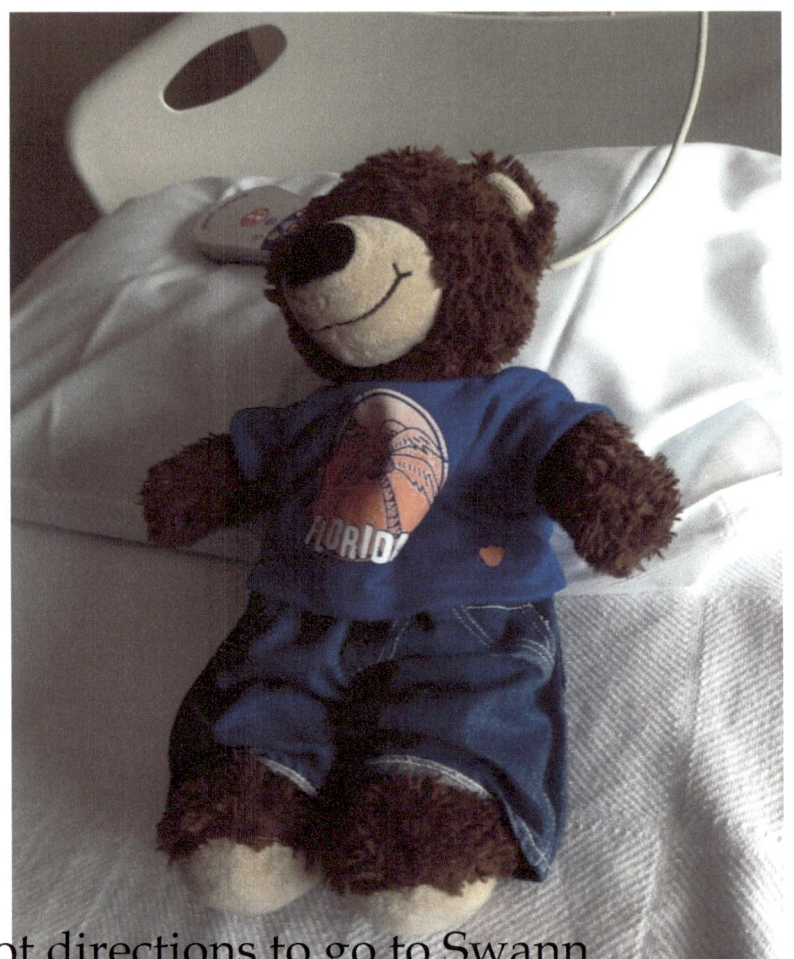

We got directions to go to Swann six, and got a bed in room 600. We are the only ones in here so far. Mom is trying to find out if we can get the same room all weekend, or if we have to sign in every day. Even so, she seems more relaxed. We have an alarm set on our phone and we are hoping for a nap.

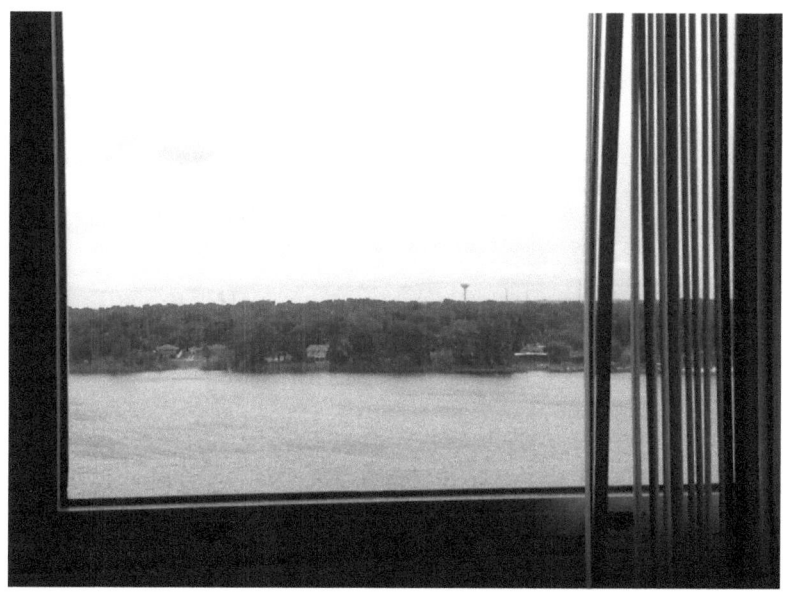

Mom put the weather Channel on our television, so we can keep an eye on Irma. And it is a category three hurricane on its come have a website, which means more of a possibility of damage. There is a voluntary evacuation. We will be here, safe my hospital for the duration. Mom works every night till Tuesday night.

The sheets on the bed are ours for the weekend. When we get up, we take our sheets and wipe down the bed the dayshift person. We need to take everything with us.

We went to the cafeteria for food. It turns out, we get three free meals a day, up to five dollars. We got a hotdog, mashed potatoes, and a large sprite which came out to be 4.60. Go mom!

We made a great lady from the Cath Lab named Beth. Here moms each other in passing in the mornings, but it was first time they talked.

I hope we have a good night tonight and that everyone got in safely. I have heard the doors closed at six, so we are officially in.

It is a slow night so far. Hospital is shut down from the outside so there is no one left in the emergency room. Dayshift is asleep or getting ready to sleep. Night shift is working, like we are. It has been a good night so far, four of us in the laundry room. We even had a visit from Andrew and Thomas. That was fun. It is as if everyone is determined to make this as pleasant as possible and we are grateful for that.

Nightshift gets free food at 11. We need to make sure to eat well and take care of ourselves.

We have a hospital called a code green, which means extreme weather. The hurricane is at the Florida Keys.

We are in a flash flood watch until Monday afternoon.

Lunchtime. We got a fish fillet and french fries and a large sprite. He was 585, but we only pay $.55. I was worried that the hurricane will cost us for food; but we are OK. The night is still going well and I am pleased that Mom is OK. I hope everyone else is OK too.

Sunday
9/10/2017

We should start getting the bad weather at seven in the morning when you're trying to go to sleep is when the weather is expected to get bad. I hope we feel secure enough to sleep and that we went safely, rested and ready to work.

Got to bed, got another roommate. We slept well.

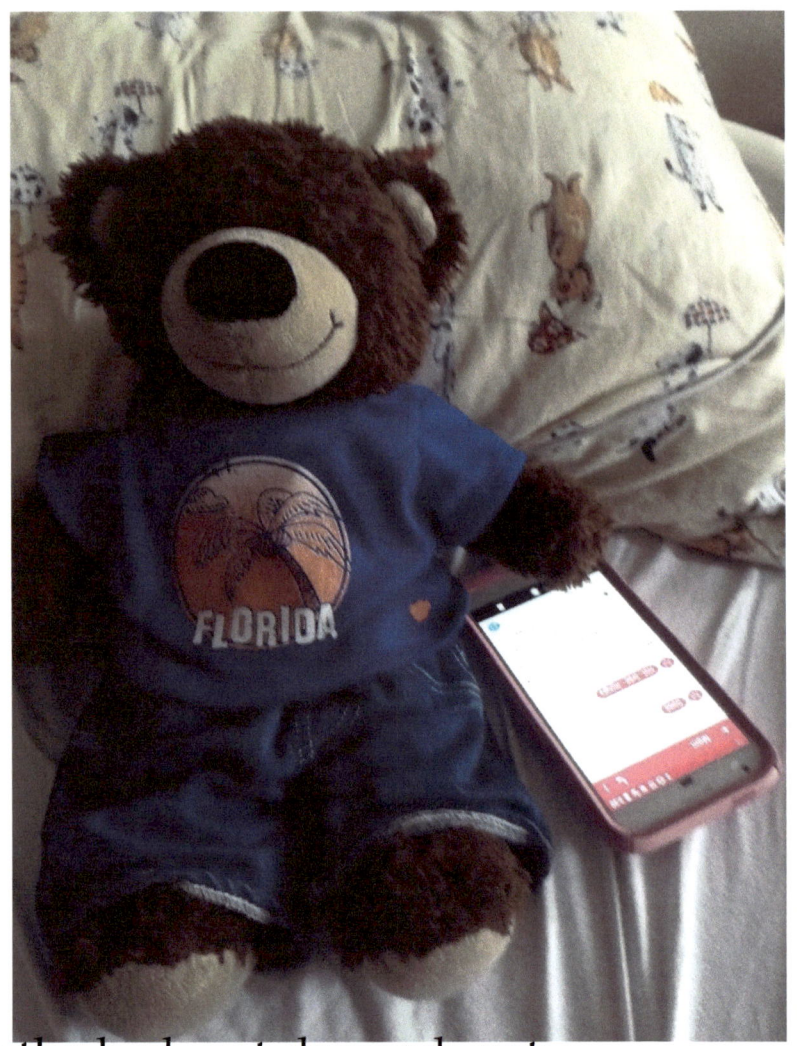

Clean the bed, got dressed, got dinner – rigatoni, green beans, and a large Sprite -.44. We are at work 1800 hrs., let Sharon go home. It is very rainy out. Thomas is here and Tracy is coming. It is night two of three, or four of six for the week.

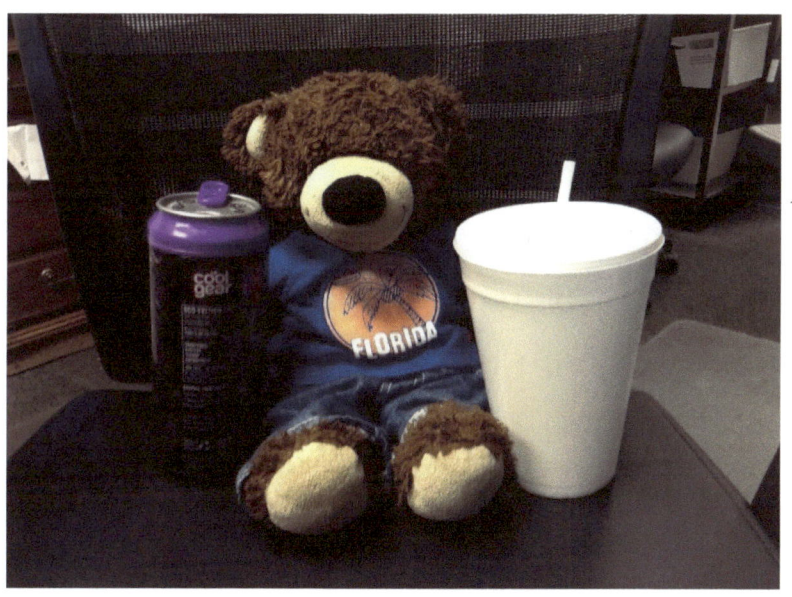

Two boards came off the windows at home.

Every year Mom has said she was afraid of working a code green. Now she's doing it, calmly and methodically, relatively speaking. She is taking it as well as any other day. I am proud of her. Keep up being strong, Mom. I will be by your side the whole way. Still, there's much hurricane to go.

When's our 55 mph in Winterhaven per our local weather. We have a long list of patients off please, we are doing the best weekend, same as always.

2141 - A large lightning flash outside and the lights flicker inside you. Let's continue to flicker on and off, off and on.

Mom got her flashlight from Swann six. Just something to help me feel better, and her. Let us hope we do not need it.

2211 - Irma is going through Polk

County. The eye is over Arcadia. We might get the eye by midnight. When is 62 mph, forty degrees.

2319 - lunch, Ravioli, Sprite, and an apple - .35

2340 - The eye of the hurricane is over Polk County. We have water leaking into some corners and we are losing ceiling tiles. The windows in the stairwells are bending. People are storm watching in the stairwells.

2347 - The lights have flickered several times and they are out. We have a tornado watch until midnight.

Monday
9/10/2017

0017 - A tornado is coming in our direction. Power is out in the cafeteria and we are on generator power.

0021 - The eye is upon us.

0547 - The generators died in the teles are out. I hate those dicks or coworkers that we have our lantern on. All of street side has been notified. Things have gotten interesting.

0640 - In bed. It is warm and dark. Wish us a good sleep and a safe

hospital

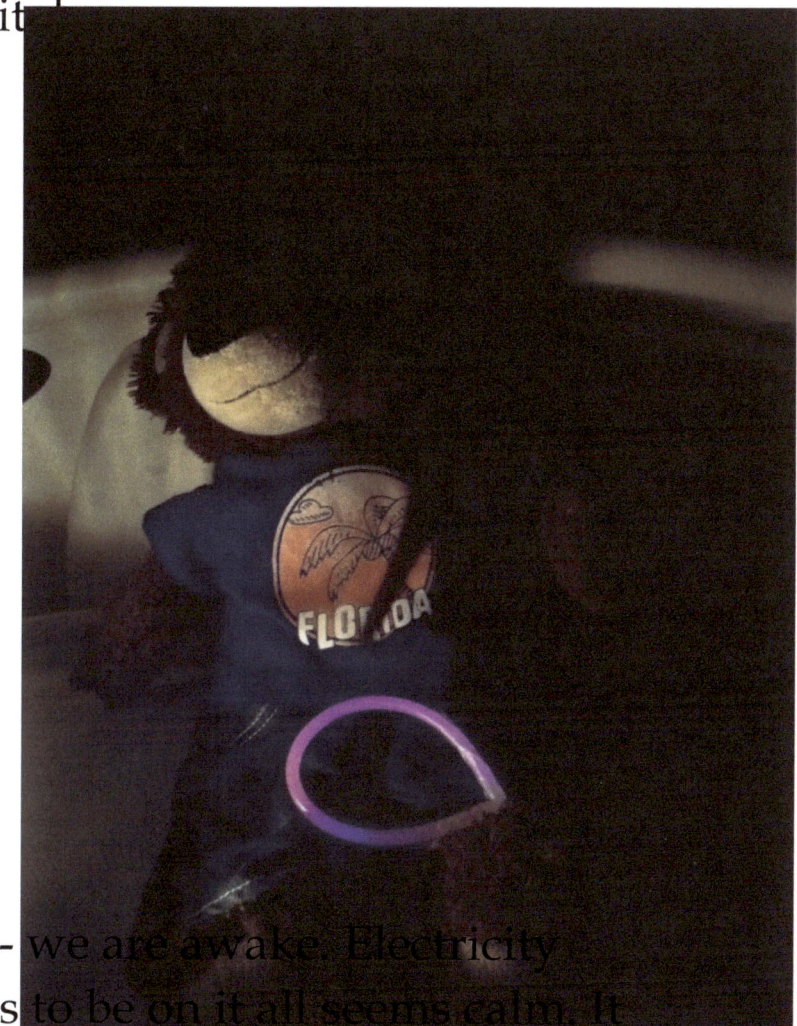

1500 - we are awake. Electricity seems to be on it all seems calm. It is day three of three of the lock in and day five of six of moms long week.

We are taking our time getting dressed. We got dressed, pack our things and strip the bed for the last time.

We dropped our clothes off and same here, then to the basement for food. 544. The code green must be over. Salsberry steak and mashed potatoes with a large Sprite.

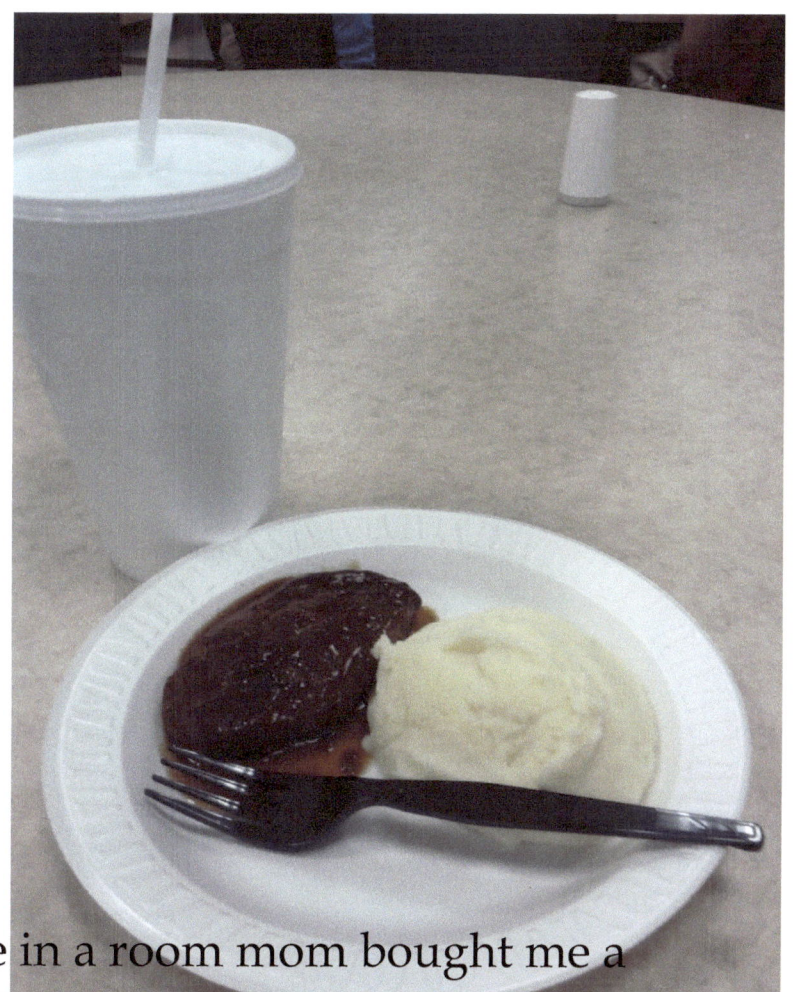

While in a room mom bought me a Woody costume from eBay because she has a friend in me. We take our food upstairs so we can get to work. Paul is already there.

After this weekend, Monday is relatively tame. There are many patients and no doubt we will all get full screens. They lifted the code green and curfew at 1500 hrs. we are free to go home in the morning. What

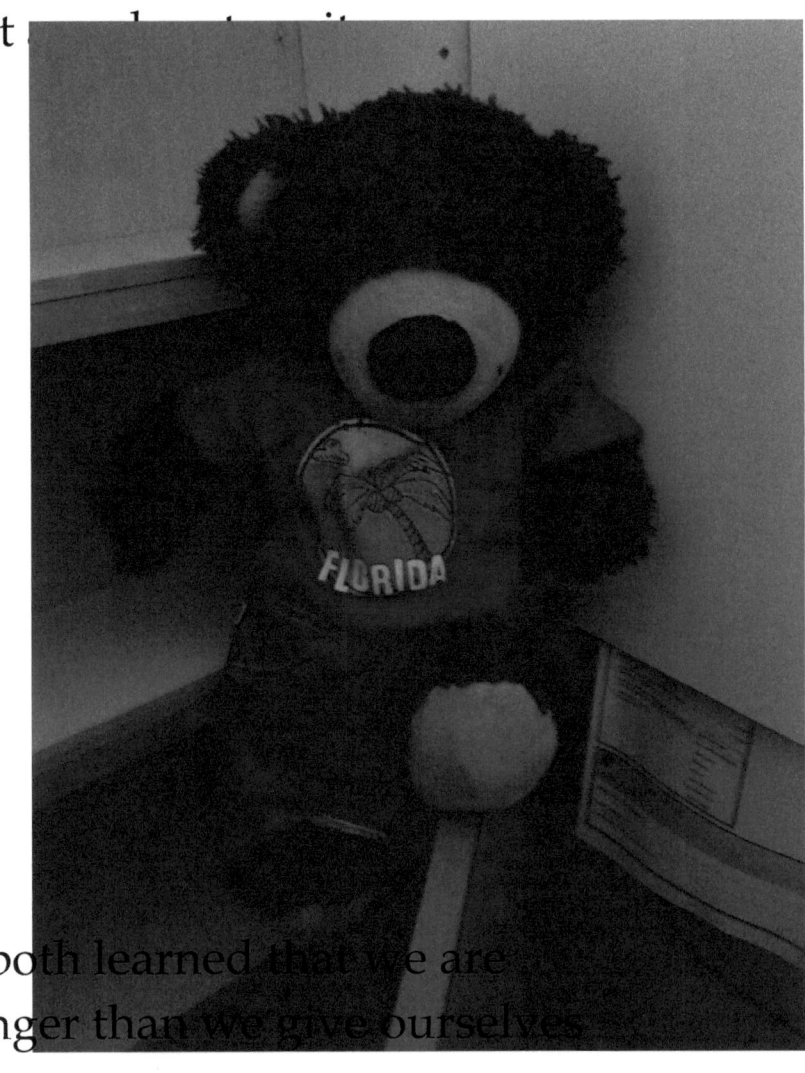

We both learned that we are stronger than we give ourselves

credit for. I was amazed by Mom's ability to put her fear aside to care for her patients, and get the sleep she needed. Together we outlasted a hurricane. That is pretty awesome.

Tuesday
9/12/2017

One more night of work, but we get to sleep at home. The cats miss us, and we missed them. Our own bed is so comfortable.

Mom works for one more night, then we are off for eight nights. She went to work, I stayed home to compare notes with the bedroom crew.

I hope everyone is safe in the aftermath of the storm. It will take time to rebuild, but we are already over the worst of it. I have faith that we will have the strength to go on.

www.ingramcontent.com/pod-product-compliance
Lightning Source LLC
Chambersburg PA
CBHW041948240526
45473CB00036B/2785